New Day, New Me was written to help those of us
in recovery—and everyone is in recovery from
something—who are developing, strengthening,
or renewing a relationship with God. We learn it's
essential to depend on someone, or something,
other than ourselves. Daily devotions, prayer,
and meditation time are critical components of
maintaining our sobriety and building a strong
foundation with God. Just as our physical bodies need
daily nourishment, we also need spiritual food every
day to withstand life on life's terms.

This devotional journal incorporates scriptural
references along with practical, spiritual teachings
which we can apply to our everyday circumstances.

RECOVERY—WHY NOT?

The LORD makes firm the steps
of the one who delights in him;
though he may stumble, he will not fall,
for the LORD upholds him with his hand (Psalm 37:23-24, NIV).

Everyone on this planet is recovering from something. A mustard seed of willingness is all that is needed to take a baby step out of addiction and into God's unique witness protection program. Fixed upon our next fix, the only peace we thought possible was death as the enemy kept confirming our ticket to the slimy pit of hell. During life's most violent storm, our ship's mast and sail were ripped away. We soon found ourselves hanging onto a piece of wreckage, while sharks circled about. Nothing, absolutely nothing, could help us except God. He responded to our cry, lifted us from our impending watery grave, and enrolled us into His accelerated program of faith, grace, and mercy.

When the light bulb of God's truth begins to shine, we discover there are four choices: jail, mental institution, death, or recovery. We might as well try recovery, as the other three will always be waiting for us! God has a purpose for our lives; He desires us to be of service to others. In so doing, we remain in touch with who we were—selfish and ungrateful. He is delighted when we allow Him to love the unlovable through us.

Why do we struggle with humbling ourselves under God's mighty hand, when it is His hand that upholds us? Our past is forgiven, our present has meaning, and our future is secure.

Lord, I pray for your grace to search, give up, and throw away whatever is blocking your blessings to me. I praise you for this season of recovery. Amen.

PSALM 40:2; 1 PETER 5:6; ECCLESIASTES 3:6

NEW DAY, NEW ME

Devotions of Acceptance, Courage, and Surrender

BELLE
GIFTS

RECOVERY JOURNAL

Belle City Gifts
Racine, WI 53403
Bellecitygifts.com

Belle City Gifts is an imprint of BroadStreet Publishing Group, LLC.

NEW DAY, NEW ME:

Devotions of Acceptance, Courage, and Surrender

© 2015 Mike Shea

ISBN 978-1-4245-4975-7

Cover and interior design by Chris Garborg | www.garborgdesign.com

Printed in China

What am I willing to do to show myself, and others, I want to recover?

It's Possible

"Seek the Kingdom of God above all else, and live righteously, and he will give you everything you need" (MATTHEW 6:33, NLT).

Is recovery possible after multiple treatments and jail time? God's promise seems a bit reckless—He will give us everything we need if we seek Him first. He makes the impossible possible! We spent years in the kingdom of me, and were tricked into thinking we were in total control. We need a bit of faith, tiny as a mustard seed, to begin our pilgrimage to freedom. Our life has been a total mess, and numerous attempts to "do things our way" took us to some dark and dismal places. God invites us to leave our throne and kneel before His.

Prayer to the Father is essential. Humbly invite Him to fill you with faith and hope. You seek the Father's Kingdom each time you depend on Him and ask for help. Recovery is possible if you believe! The Heavenly Father never gives up on you. When today's problems seem unbearable and using again comes into your mind, listen to the Holy Spirit whisper gently, "with God, all things are possible."

By God's abundant grace, and with radical trust, take a step out of the impossible and leave the darkness you once believed was home. Enter His light; it's so bright you need special order Son-glasses. Bask in His radiant and unconditional love, and ask for His help with your doubt.

Lord, I do believe you'll give me what I need; help me not to doubt. A new life of freedom from addiction is possible, because with you all things are possible. Amen.

MARK 9:22-23; MATTHEW 19:26

Am I convinced that I have to work a comprehensive
program in order to recover?

_____

_____

_____

_____

_____

_____

_____

_____

_____

_____

_____

_____

_____

_____

_____

_____

_____

IT'S YOUR SEASON FOR RECOVERY

For everything there is a season, and a time for every matter under heaven
(ECCLESIASTES 3:1, ESV).

We are witness to a garden's different and necessary seasons. In spring we sow the seed, fertilize, and water; in early summer we pull weeds and water; later in the summer we harvest, eat fresh, and water some more; in autumn we plant flower bulbs for the coming spring; and in winter the soil rests while we enjoy the harvest.

A garden without water will have no harvest. A recovery program becomes lifeless without Living Water to nourish and empower new life. When we're thirsty, Jesus says, "Come and drink." The weeds of old belief and "doing it my way" combined with laziness reap a negative harvest: no mentor, fewer meetings, and a self-centered and critical outlook. The constant "you ain't gonna tell me what to do" attitude restricts the very grace and mercy which fertilize growth. If we're lazy with our garden of recovery, we'll be back on the prison chain-gang of hard labor in a relapse.

As a garden thirsts for water, trust that your thirst is only met by the Son of God. Each of us are in different seasons with a unique opportunity to embrace or let go, turn into or turn away, listen or speak, receive Living Water or stay in the desert, and keep going or give up. God declares we're worthy to keep moving forward. Trust Him a bit more intensely and experience the harvest.

Lord, I pray for grace to be thirsty for your Living Water and the courage to drink it.
I'm grateful for your deposit in me. I can draw from you during my season of need.
Amen.

JOHN 4:10, 7:37; GALATIANS 6:9

What steps can I take to ensure a successful recovery?

TIME TO WORD UP

In the beginning was the Word, and the Word was with God, and the Word was God
(JOHN 1:1, NKJV).

Early on, as we dare stick and stay to check out what a new life in recovery looks like, we are brought face to face with the majesty and power of the One who reached down during our critical time of need to save us from certain destruction. It's a huge challenge for many of us to even fathom we're worthy of God's unending grace and tender mercies, and that's okay—because we aren't! God is the One who made us worthy. Only with Him can we become the person He says we are.

It's our time to discover why we are, who we are, and whose we are. There is an obstruction before us that can be a great hindrance to tapping into His power; we need to get to know the living and active Word. The only path to Him is picking up the Bible, His bag of seeds to fulfill our needs, and begin making deposits into our spirit. When we open ourselves to the Word with radical abandon, we soon learn He knows what we need and don't need. In a light-bulb moment, we no longer need to let circumstances control us.

Our Heavenly Father wants to sanctify us. This gives us an overwhelming, amazing revelation that God Himself desires us to be His. In fact, He protected us during the darkness of addiction to get us to this moment. He set us apart to sift, shift, and re-position us into His next dimension.

O Lord, I desire to get into your Word—the truth that sets me free—
to dust off my Bible so I can know you more intimately. Thanks for your
realignment of my life, O Great Chiropractor. Amen.
HEBREWS 4:12; JOHN 17:17

What negative words of my past do I need
to exchange for God's positive words for my future?

THE WORD NEVER CHANGES

"Heaven and earth will pass away, but My words will not pass away"
(MATTHEW 24:35, NASB).

God's Word doesn't change or adapt to time or circumstance. When we accept that we cannot rise to any challenge without God, we must confront the issue within us: do we trust God? Do we believe that He can handle any situation that threatens to hurt, punish, or destroy us? It's extremely significant for recovery to get off the insane, demented roller-coaster of emotions. Each ride erodes the foundation God has been constructing for us to stand on during physical, emotional, or spiritual storms.

We no longer focus our efforts on things which rust out—are smoked up, gambled away, or drunk empty—or possessions which can be stolen. Where we once filled the empty God-space in us with everything else, the Holy Spirit now changes us by revelation that His Word is the ultimate authority—boom! It's transformation time. God's revelation to us begins our transformation. Realizing His great gift gives us the opportunity to believe in something everlasting and never-changing.

Opening His living and active Word, we clearly understand the One who created us, wrote about us. Seriously, the ultimate authority of the universe, who existed before anything was created, gives freely His God-breathed Word. Why read the Bible? Why not? We've tried everything else; we might as well check out this God deal—our life depends on it.

O Lord, I'm grateful when admitting I don't have a clue what my next step is that your Word guides me. Amen.
ISAIAH 40:8; 2 TIMOTHY 3:16-17; PSALM 119:105

Am I ready to adjust myself to the truth God says
about my past, present, and future?

How Near the Bible?

I will study your commandments
and reflect on your ways (PSALM 119:15, NLT).

Will we discover God's path without study or reflection on the Word? Simply and unequivocally—no! He lights our path, marks it, and gives us grace to walk on it. He also gives us strength to endure, tender mercies to continue, and showers of blessings along the way while preparing a mansion for our eternal destination.

Abba Father already knows what His path for us looks like. He will guide us into our future, declare our identity as one of His children, and reveal His will for us. He created us to choose Him and to walk on His path. The Word ignites our very purpose. It prospers in and through us. God already gave us an A+ for taking the Jesus' Honors Class when we opened, read, and studied the Bible.

How near and dear has the Bible been to you? If there's dust on the front cover thick enough to use your finger to write "Read Me," there's no shame—just wipe off the dust and start reading. The enemy of our souls will do all in his power to keep the Word on the shelf and off our lips.

Lord, thanks for your grace to receive and welcome your Word to be implanted
and rooted in me. I desire your courage and strength to become a doer of
your Word so I may serve you. Amen.
PROVERBS 2:8; ISAIAH 55:11; ROMANS 10:8-10

Am I willing to take a chance and begin to read the Bible?

THE ENEMY'S ARROWS ARE TOXIC

In all circumstances take up the shield of faith, with which you can extinguish all the flaming darts of the evil one (EPHESIANS 6:16, ESV).

On the journey of recovery, many of us believe that after we have dealt with resentment, anger, or guilt from our past, it's been taken care of—gone. Yet, we continue experiencing moments of pain and shame that begin to flow over us. In a flash, something pops into our minds that we thought was removed. When plagued by a persistent attack concerning the same issue, it's an opportunity to confront a stronghold.

The fiery arrows of the enemy will stick on and in us. If not dealt with on a timely basis, the toxicity of poison from these darts places us at great risk. Our shield of faith allows us to believe the unseen. We can't see the arrows hit, yet we can know when things which come at us are not from God. The confidence we have in our Heavenly Father encourages us to ask Him to reveal the poisons from our past that still stick. These poisons, if allowed to stay, will kill us.

It is essential to have spiritual accountability in our lives. We need someone to let us know when there are flaming arrows sticking in our back. Their intensity is in direct proportion to our faith. We have to believe God will intervene, provide guidance, and remove any blockage of generational curses. God's truth and light are more than we can ever hope for, and beyond what we can ever pray for, exceeding our wildest expectations of Him.

O Lord, I'm thankful your Word is alive and powerful, and that every knee in the universe will bow before you, including mine. I desire your faith to be fearless in using my shield to defend, your Word as a sword, and your cross for deliverance.

Amen.

ROMANS 14:11

What is currently in me that needs to be removed?

Strongholds

The weapons we fight with are not the weapons of the world. On the contrary, they have divine power to demolish strongholds (2 Corinthians 10:4, niv).

The mighty weapon we use against the spirit of heaviness is putting on our garments of praise. In doing this we become aware of the strongholds Satan has set up to conduct operations that take over our lives—seeds of destruction he invited us to plant in our garden at an early age. The enemy's goal is to harden our hearts.

As we believed Satan's lies, we never clearly understood our emotional reaction to situations; when we wanted to react the right way, we found ourselves responding the wrong way. We all have strongholds in our lives: fear assaults areas of rest and trust; addictions and sexual perversions affect love of self and others; rejection comes against who we see in the mirror; confusion squeezes out wisdom for good decisions; and pride wants to control.

The enemy's ultimate lie is to impersonate us to ourselves so we believe we are the evil we hate. Satan uses the words out of our mouths to speak death. The truth is we are the beloved of Jesus—the adopted sons and daughters of the Most High God. He protects us and gives us grace to endure the temptation to go back into the chaos of addiction.

O Lord, thanks for never taking away my inheritance in you and always loving me in spite of my human imperfections. I'm so grateful you're the same yesterday, today, and tomorrow. Amen.

John 8:44; Romans 7:15, 24-25; Hebrews 13:8

Why do I find it hard to recognize that the Bible
is a weapon given me to fight the enemy?

THROUGH HIM AND IN HIM

I can do all things through Him who strengthens me (PHILIPPIANS 4:13, NASB).

It's a tough day when another step forward seems impossible, and we are at the end of our rope. This is a good thing because our efforts stop and God's strength begins. Even while pleading to God for help, our stubborn flesh demands more time at the pity party. It's difficult to quit looking in the rear view mirror, rehearsing past hurts and resentments; yet, if we don't stop and look ahead to the path set before us, we will run off the road and crash for the umpteenth time. Do we grab God's secure lifeline, or not?

Only with child-like faith do we grasp onto Jesus' robe and experience the Holy Father's breath of life delivering, refreshing, and reassuring us. God desires intimate fellowship with us. He doesn't want us to smother or block our access to Him with twisted thinking. We call upon our Savior, Jesus, to intercede for us, and through Him we have access to the Father.

Our situation might not change, but the Holy Spirit empowers us to change how we deal with it. This is about progress, not perfection. We're learning to embrace the Spirit's fire within us and accept ourselves as we truly are: poor in spirit, and in need of His grace. In Him, we can do all things. In Him, we have one more day free of addiction.

O Lord, thanks that all things are from you and come through you.
To you belongs the glory forever. Amen.
HEBREWS 2:18, 7:25; 1 THESSALONIANS 5:16-19; ROMANS 11:36

Why is it easy to give God everything when I have nothing to give,
and so hard to give Him anything when I have something?

CONFORM? ABSOLUTELY NOT!

Don't copy the behavior and customs of this world, but let God transform you into a new person by changing the way you think. Then you will learn to know God's will for you, which is good and pleasing and perfect (ROMANS 12:2, NLT).

In this world, we're battered and bruised by what we see and hear, and we're tricked by the enemy to settle for much less than what God has for us. We didn't have a clue while in the long, silent line of conformity; we were absorbed into a life centered on how we felt. Though moments of clarity gave momentary hope, we were lacking the discipline needed to change on our own even when admitting we were powerless. In the battlefield of our minds, our recovery is greatly threatened by conforming to how we feel; we're worried about what others think, or we're paralyzed over external circumstances.

We're so prone to jump at that which hurts us, and hesitant to go all in for what helps us. We need to learn to love ourselves and others. It's essential to know we're dealing with issues that were already in us before our active addiction. The "why" behind the "what" is simply that we medicated the pain, shame, and guilt that were already present. God never gave up on us.

This is strictly an inside job. We might need an occasional push and shove by someone to get to the place we need to be. We're rebels; we will never let anyone shove something down our throats. We respond to someone whose actions speak loudly—show me, don't tell me! We were never afraid of the wrong things, so why are we afraid to recover?

O Lord, I ask for your grace to fix my thoughts on what is true, honorable, right, pure, lovely, and admirable. Amen.

ACTS 20:35; PHILIPPIANS 4:8

Why do I allow myself to conform to my circumstances and feelings
and not allow God to raise me above my circumstances?

A TIME FOR MILK

You have been Christians a long time now, and you ought to be teaching others, but instead you have dropped back to the place where you need someone to teach you all over again the very first principles in God's Word. You are like babies who can drink only milk, not old enough for solid food
(HEBREWS 5:12, TLB).

We need to be on guard to recognize our flesh invites us to go back to what's familiar whenever stress, anxiety, or enemy attacks come at us. As we journey down the path of recovery, the levels and dimensions experienced on a daily basis can fluctuate. As we stick and stay, we experience growth. We understand even more deeply when we admit we were one of the crafty people in our deceitful scheming.

Truth spoken in love is effective, but truth spoken in criticism and judgment is not. The only reason we're anything is because of Him—the author of love. We're the beloved of Jesus. He proved His love for us by His actions on the cross. When we were alone, abandoned, lost, and near death, He knew exactly what we needed to experience His love. It is unconditional, always present, and never withdrawn.

We are all His kids—adopted children of the Most High God—and by His grace, we're open to learning about Him all over again. We need to set aside past experiences with religion and church. We can start fresh and new; we get up into Jesus' lap with our Sippy cups and learn His truth.

O Lord, I need your grace to accept being spoon-fed again, especially when I want a steak sandwich. Amen.
EPHESIANS 4:14; 1 JOHN 5:1

What necessary actions can I take to get me back to the basics of my faith?

When the Heat Is Turned Up

These trials will show that your faith is genuine. It is being tested as fire tests and purifies gold—though your faith is far more precious than mere gold. So when your faith remains strong through many trials, it will bring you much praise and glory and honor on the day when Jesus Christ is revealed to the whole world
(1 PETER 1:7, NLT).

We've been made to do more than just survive. When we think a little more work will change our situation, Jesus reminds us we just need a little more faith. We usually want to receive all of God's good stuff while sitting in a recliner with our feet up. But without persevering and embracing the testing and trials which come at us on a daily basis, we would never discover what we're capable of.

What's our response when we're in the furnace with the heat turned up? Why me and not them? Why would a loving God allow this? God, haven't I been through enough? It's all hissy-fits when it's about us! As we dare to embrace our Father's gift of unconditional love, His breath of grace breathes into us His truth: He uses all our past experiences, pain, difficulties, disasters, and even Satan's attacks to build character and to kindle our excitement to know each new day holds great promise. In Him, our futures are secure.

When addicted, we pursued the lie of the enemy. We should focus on being refined by short term pain to receive long term gain; it's more fulfilling than the enemy's short term gain with long term pain!

O Lord, thanks for refining me for your purpose.
I see your bright light in the dark night. Amen.
ROMANS 5:3; PSALM 16:8

When my faith is tested, can it be trusted?

Offense

A person's wisdom yields patience;
it is to one's glory to overlook an offense (PROVERBS 19:11, NIV).

Jesus died to set us free from the list of laws and regulations that the enemy uses to condemn us. The struggle within is the conviction and desire to do what's right, yet, often, our flesh overrules. One area the devil uses to twist us up into tiny knots is the area of offense.

We have the opportunity to be offended by everything and everyone: mom and dad, family, origin, home, correction, rebuke, bullying, lack of recognition, and the list goes on. We're extremely sensitive people, capable of pulling offense out of one sentence in an entire conversation. We're inadequate and inferior. The driver on the freeway who cuts in tightly is something we take seriously. Offense is all around us!

We must recognize what we are really struggling with. When in church, a Bible study, or a meeting, we're tempted to be offended because it's taking too long. When receiving counsel or truthful correction, we get offended at the very person who is trying to speak words of life into us. We're even offended by those we love. This is how easily we get entrapped by the enemy. None of this offense has anything to do with others; the spirit of offense is from the pit of hell and it's stealing from us. The offense we experience begins inside of us—the issue ish-you!

O Lord, help me with the many times I feel offended by words said and not said,
by actions done or not done. Amen.
ROMANS 7:15; EPHESIANS 6:12

When people are trying to help me, why do I feel belittled and offended?

Offended

"Blessed is he who is not offended because of Me" (MATTHEW 11:6, NKJV).

We take inventory to accept our faith is weak concerning certain situations, people, or places—spiritual red flags of caution. Clarity comes while accepting the truth that our dispute is not with others; we're actually judging and arguing with ourselves. Our faith grows when around other survivors of the deep depths of hopelessness we experienced. They build us up instead of tearing us down. As God empowers us to meet those He brings into our lives just as they are, we learn to embrace ourselves where we are.

John the Baptist was in prison confused, offended, and wasting away wondering why. Jesus spoke to John, through His disciples, of miracles which proved His identity. While alone in a dark dungeon, John may have been offended because Jesus seemed too busy to rescue him, or he perhaps doubted the divine purpose for his life. Jesus knew the root of John's question, and He hadn't forgotten about John or His purpose for his life.

God is no respecter of persons. He isn't going to lose His reputation over us. When God gives us an assignment, He is responsible for it. The great task before us is to embrace being the least in the kingdom of heaven, and guard ourselves against being offended.

O Lord, reveal offense in me and lead me in your everlasting way.
I desire to live my life not offended by myself or others. Amen.

ROMANS 14:1; EZEKIEL 33:10; MATTHEW 11:2-11; JOHN 1:23, 3:30; PSALM 139:24

How do I respond when people offend me?

Time for a New Mind

You have heard about him and were taught in him... to put off your old self, which belongs to your former manner of life and is corrupt through deceitful desires, and to be renewed in the spirit of your minds (EPHESIANS 4:21-23, ESV).

It's truly a God moment when our child-like faith kicks in. The bat we beat ourselves up with is laid down and we declare, "Lord, our heart's desire is to seek you, listen and hear your words of life, develop our personal relationship with you, and receive your grace to empower us. Our sincere desire is learning acceptance of self, and of others. I'm going to be me, and you can be you!"

We have put together three, six, and nine months of sobriety, only to crash and burn for the fourth, seventh, and eleventh time. Our only hope is the God of faith, hope, and love—and we definitely fit His only requirement needed for a new life. We are broken, poor in spirit, and humbled enough to say, "I need you, Abba Father, for my next breath and step because without you, I'm toast." The bottom line is that Jesus declared our worthiness at His cross. He made us righteous before His Father, took the hit for us, and when we were walking the last mile to the execution chamber, He called the warden and gave us a full pardon.

We need to know this is life or death. We know we've got another relapse in us (some may be planning one right now), yet we need to ask with every ounce of courage, "Do we have another recovery?" None of us are guaranteed tomorrow. It is our turn, our time for a new mind. If we wonder or question whether the renewal of our mind has begun, we can emphatically say we're already on the pilgrimage to learning what God's will for us is—and this is pleasing and perfect!

Lord, I'm grateful recovery is beginning to break loose for me. Thanks for the wisdom to know the only time it's okay to worry is when I'm in charge. Amen.

ROMANS 12:1-2

When is the last time I really thought about what I'm thinking about?

A Fool to Become Wise

Be faithful to guard the sweet harmony of the Holy Spirit among you in the bonds of peace, so that you will be one body and one spirit, as you were all called into the same glorious hope of divine destiny (EPHESIANS 4:3-4, TPT).

Paul spoke powerfully to the Church of Corinth about relying only on the Holy Spirit. It's crucial that we trust it's our time and season to receive a fresh Spirit. The Holy Spirit gives us revelation or disclosure of divine truth. In our spirit we know of our reserved ticket to heaven. We stumble over our reasoning and intellect which cannot fathom the depth of God's great love and His plan of salvation.

Because spiritual truths can't be explained by human knowledge, the words sound foolish when we attempt to figure them out in our minds. This goes both ways. The wisdom of the world is foolishness to God. This is why it's such a struggle; our flesh demands to be in control while the enemy comes to steal God's wisdom from us. Our prideful, egotistical self absolutely hates the idea that we are foolish without God.

This is about relationship, not religion. We have an Advocate who testifies: we are forgiven, our sins are removed, and our slates are wiped clean. Distraction and confusion invite us to either look at our past (shame, guilt, regret) or to the future (anxiety, control). The Holy Spirit leads us into truth, which for today is simply, "My beloved, hold onto my hand, and walk with me, your past is gone and your future secure."

Lord, thanks for wisdom to know any problem between you and me is due to my disobedience. I pray for the simplicity to hold your hand and enjoy your presence.
Amen.

1 CORINTHIANS 2:2-4, 10, 3:18-19; HEBREWS 10:17

Why do I have a hard time admitting I know nothing
when God knows everything?

Remember No More

Guilt screams that we've made another mess while shame declares we are the mess! The enemy digs our guilt and shame out of his bag of strategies to entice us to agree with his counterfeit against being forgiven. We know it's shame when we feel defective, inadequate, and unworthy. Out of our lips come the words, "I'm so ashamed," "I'm stupid," "I never say or do the right thing," or, "I'm a failure." Sometimes others speak shame over us: "You'll never amount to anything," "you're a troublemaker," "you're a quitter," "no one can ever trust you," or, "it's always your fault."

We're one of the world's great sabotage experts in self-destruction—imperfect and defective since the Garden of Eden. Guilt is what we did; we confess it to God and He forgives. Shame is who we are; we repent and discover our shame was nailed to Jesus' cross. This is progress, not perfection. We walk with Him into freedom and remember what He has told us in His Word. Daily check-ups on our spiritual condition are essential. We need people to encourage and remind us to keep moving forward.

The enemy's lies, our thoughts, and wrongful words spoken are dismantled and erased as the Holy Spirit reveals the truth. He even intercedes for us when we have no words. He convicts and empowers us to change. Instead of doing what we want when we want to, we do what He desires us to do when He nudges us to do it. It's a radical transformation!

Lord, thanks for setting me free. I'm so grateful you remind me
I'm your beloved and can rest in your lap. Amen.
JOHN 8:32, 36, 14:17, 26; ROMANS 8:26

What steps can I take to accept I've made some mistakes, but I am not a mistake?

THERE IS TIME

All praise to God, the Father of our Lord Jesus Christ. It is by his great mercy that we have been born again, because God raised Jesus Christ from the dead. Now we live with great expectation, and we have a priceless inheritance—an inheritance that is kept in heaven for you, pure and undefiled, beyond the reach of change and decay
(1 PETER 1:3-4, NLT).

No matter how wrong things may seem, the simplicity of our recovery begins to seep into our mind and heart as we embrace His truth which sets us free from yesterday, today, and tomorrow. As confusion, chaos, worry, and fear rise from the pit of hell, we stand firm. Our victim mentality is being replaced by a victor mindset.

Jesus reveals His heart—His love and forgiveness—and empowers us by His Spirit to know we're now His children with a new identity in Him. We were once lost, now adopted; guilty, now forgiven; in darkness, now in the living light of the Son of God; dead in sin, now spiritually alive. We are empowered to confront our flesh and say no to the devil. When we fall, we dust ourselves off and get back up. A storm hits; we endure. When He speaks, we listen, and we never give up. "Our greatest weakness is giving up. The most certain way to success is to try one more time" (Thomas Edison).

A huge issue for us is the thought of having lost so much—especially time. Our addiction has burned bridges involving children, family, friends, or work, and we wonder if there's time to rebuild and reconnect. Time seems to have passed by so quickly. Sun rises; wake up. Sun sets; sleep. Spring thaws and flowers bloom; winter freezes and gloomy doom. Days seem to be quickening as morning becomes night during its relentless march to a new year. God's truth declares there is time to get our inside world put right regardless of age or the years we think have been wasted. He is making all things new.

Lord, thanks for your gift of child-like faith, and your truth which says the next years of my life will be the best. Amen.

1 PETER 5:9; ECCLESIASTES 3:1

Why do I have a hard time believing the rest of my life can be the best of my life?

STAY OR RUN

As water reflects the face, so one's life reflects the heart (PROVERBS 27:19, NIV).

In recovery, we begin to realize we're not in control of anything. This journey is day by day, based on our willingness and obedience. It is great comfort to learn the outcome of the war we've struggled with all these years has been already decided at Jesus' cross. By God's unlimited grace and tender mercies, we can access His power and resources to live the abundant life He says we can.

Our tiniest faith applied diligently and consistently can move mountains which block our path and kill the giants waiting to ambush us along the way. We show great faith when we trust God to help us stay clean another day.

We start on the journey by setting aside our slave mentality and accepting our new identity—adopted children of the Most High God. Our Father loves those who admit to being poor in spirit and in dire need of His grace and tender love. He is always near when we are broken. This is serious business. We can stay, recover, and embrace freedom, or run, relapse, and be imprisoned.

Lord, thanks for being near to my broken heart and for protecting me.
Create in me a clean heart. Amen.
MATTHEW 17:20; PSALMS 31:14, 51:10, 73:26

Why am I struggling with expressing to others that I want to quit,
when I know I need to quit in order to recover?

Our Shepherds

"I will give you shepherds after my own heart, who will feed you with knowledge and understanding" (JEREMIAH 3:15, ESV).

This is an absolute truth: we need people daily to help, guide, and assist us in recovery. None of us came in on a winning streak. Our best thinking got us into police cars, waiting on the corner in driving rain, living in a car at a casino parking lot, drinking in secret, stealing pain meds, or hiding in a closet when the doorbell rang. Our lives were a continual medication of the deep pain and shame within; in fact, we had no life!

When beginning our recovery journey, we learn to follow God by observing the example of others who are following God's guidance and direction. The disciples of Jesus were taught with knowledge and understanding. They were ordinary human beings who became effective only after Jesus sent His Spirit into them. The fruit of the Holy Spirit is evident in those empowered by the Spirit: how they live invites our child-like faith to tag along and mirror their actions. We need the shade of the tree of life to keep from getting scorched by the intense heat of our past.

When we believe others are more important than ourselves, the refreshing that we experience encourages us to know God will also refresh others through us, and we're blessed. We can't keep what we have unless we give it away! God will bless us with shepherds after His own heart if we ask.

Lord, thanks for allowing me to be refreshed by others.
When I refresh others, you bless me. I'm so grateful for all the shepherds
you have given and will continue to give me. Amen.

PROVERBS 11:25, 30

What is it going to take for me to accept that God
has put people in my life for my own benefit?

HIS GIFTS WILL KEEP US SOBER

He set his seal of ownership on us, and put his Spirit in our hearts as a deposit, guaranteeing what is to come (2 CORINTHIANS 1:22, NIV).

God's seal guarantees we belong to Him and assures us of receiving benefits with an eternal bonus. His deposit of Himself into us totally, unequivocally, never ceasing, and without reservation declares throughout the universe that salvation is ours. Our benefits include a new mind and heart, no memory of sin, an advocate, a teacher, peace, a seal, a guarantee of promises to come, conviction, and God speaking through us. These benefits are not of this world!

God also throws in gifts: wise advice, special knowledge, great faith, healing, miracles, prophecy, discernment, speaking in unknown languages, and interpreting what's been said. Where do we start? Once again, we learn these gifts from being around others with gifts. We discover these gifts are in us waiting to be developed. When feeling stretched beyond everything we've known, it's okay. Many relapses happen when recovering addicts are too comfortable. God's special gifts empower us to enjoy another day of life.

What's the difference between the progression of our addiction and our faith-based recovery? There's no middle ground! We're either pursuing our new life, or falling back into our old one. This new life can be hard. We must not forget who saved us from total destruction.

Lord, I am grateful you set your seal on me, and your Spirit in me.
When I received the gift of your Son, I had no clue you would gift me
with so much more of yourself. Thank you. Amen.
HEBREWS 10:15-17; JOHN 16:8; MATTHEW 10:10; 1 CORINTHIANS 12:8-10

Why do I feel like I have nothing to offer?

TRIALS: A REFINER'S FIRE OR HELL'S FIRE?

We can rejoice, too, when we run into problems and trials, for we know that they are good for us—they help us learn to be patient (ROMANS 5:3, TLB).

It stretches us beyond our wildest imagination to consider trials a joy. Our initial reaction is one of trying to reason and figure out what and why something is happening. Intellectual dissection is a dead-end without answers, and we are frustrated by our double-mindedness. The enemy is having a field day attempting to get us to argue with ourselves. Scripture says trials will show up; we shouldn't be surprised when they do. Some of us at this very moment are facing trials which seem overwhelming. Red flags and pop-ups from the past assault us intensely.

We're making progress when we know that problems and trials help us learn to endure. This strengthens us to get through it—to get to the blessing on the other side. Endurance is about surviving regardless of the problem. As we persevere and mature, fear, distrust, and anger are slowly replaced by love, trust, and calmness.

Whose report do we believe concerning problems and trials? A refiner's fire, which is a blessing, or hell's fire, which is a curse? God chose us to be warriors on the battlefield going forth believing, to the best of our ability, that our trial is pure joy. Our Father desires us to mature and accept these trials as opportunities to grow in trusting Him. He never gives us more than we can endure. He's got our backs!

Lord, thanks for your patience when I throw a hissy-fit when problems show up;
I'm so grateful when I'm kicking, screaming, and making a fuss,
that you bring me into your lap to rest until the storm has passed. Amen.

JAMES 1:2-4; 2 PETER 1:5

Reflecting back to when I went through hard times in my life,
how have those times made me a better person?

Open His Gift

The Anointed One has set us free—not partially, but completely and wonderfully free! We must always cherish this truth and stubbornly refuse to go back into the bondage of our past (Galatians 5:1, TPT).

Christ came to set us free. We can have freedom from addiction, pride, and the enemy of our souls. Our Father's unrelenting love protected us while we were lost until we were broken, so we could admit our powerlessness. We gave up, gave in, and became willing to go all out seeking the freedom Christ had for us. Many of us were angry at God and struggled with religion.

As we began our journey of recovery, we were like babies in diapers, needing to be patient and tender with ourselves. This is a marathon of endurance and perseverance, not a sprint to instant gratification. Each new step on His path gives us added confidence of sobriety, and clean time from our addiction is actually something we embrace personally. It's important to review on a daily basis that a strong start with no foundation leads to a fall.

Jesus has personally delivered His complete gift of wholeness and healing to our doorstep—prepaid! Here lies the problem: our free will. We have the choice to accept the gift, open it, and receive His power to begin our healing. We grasp tightly our new gift and the hope God offers us without conditions, and we are encouraged.

Lord, thanks for being the anchor for my soul, and for your truth which says you won't let me go. Never. Ever. Amen.

Galatians 5:5; Hebrews 6:19

Why do I have a hard time receiving gifts from God and others?

I'm Me, Free Indeed

Anyone who belongs to Christ has become a new person.
The old life is gone; a new life has begun! (2 CORINTHIANS 5:17, NLT)

He's making us into extraordinary, new creations—renewing us day by day. God says we're no longer alcoholics, addicts, or compulsive gamblers. We need to remember when we were so broken, beat up, and powerless that we cried out to God to save us, and He did. He listened, responded, and sent His Spirit with a sledge hammer and crowbar to begin His demolition project, and rebuild us stone by stone. He's making us new. There's only one thing that has to go—everything!

God's Word says out of our mouths are spoken words of life or death. We barely survived to get to recovery and absolutely do not need to speak words of death over ourselves. What's right for us to speak about ourselves? God says we're champions; He blesses us with His grace and declares our worthiness to be made new.

We have just put our big toe into the ocean of how important words are. This is heavy-duty combat—spiritual warfare. These aren't rules or regulations; Jesus invites us to use our lips that confess His Name, to speak His living Word over us and others. Why? So we don't stumble over this straightforward message over and over again. "I'm me, and I'm free indeed."

Lord, I pray for grace to stay out of your dumpster when I want to take back stuff you've thrown away. I thought you were going to work on me with sandpaper, not a jackhammer, but I submit. Have your way with me! Amen.

JOHN 8:32; PROVERBS 8:6, 14:3; MATTHEW 15:8; HEBREWS 13:15

In what areas of my life, other than addiction, do I need freedom?

THE GOLDEN RULE

Do to others what you want them to do to you. This is the meaning of the law of Moses and the teaching of the prophets (MATTHEW 7:12, NCV).

Many who have heard "The Golden Rule" spoken by their mothers as children likely had no idea it was a summary of all that is taught in God's Word. This is a great challenge because we used to react to the Tarnished Rule: Do to others what we believed they did to us. Hurt people hurt people. Our regret and shame over our past fueled self-condemnation resulting in us being the judge, jury, and executioner of those who betrayed our trust. The enemy of our soul celebrates our path to self-destruction whenever we rehearse our hurts, justify our anger, refuse to forgive, and medicate our pain with alcohol, drugs, or rolling the dice.

When we find ourselves in Pilate's courtyard yelling, "Crucify Him!" we should look up and recognize that it isn't Jesus we see, it's us. We should be sickened by the insanity of living without hope and embracing the devil's lie of being no good. Our Father declares there is hope in Him. We need to tap into His unconditional and unfailing love for us. Then we can say, "Stop my crucifixion! Jesus already did it! It's finished!"

Our newly discovered hope encourages us to rest in Jesus' lap, and hear His loving whisper. He wants us to turn from all that is not of Him and become His children. Empowered by His Spirit, we welcome the little child in us and begin skipping joyfully on the Way.

Lord, thank you for your gift of child-like faith which replaces my thoughts of dying with your hope and your Golden Rule. Amen.

PSALM 130:7; MATTHEW 18:3-5

How does what has been done to me affect what I do to others?

God's Super Bowl

Let us not grow weary in doing what is right, for we will reap at harvest time, if we do not give up (GALATIANS 6:9, NRSV).

By God's grace we dare say, "Absolutely not this time," to our self-centered flesh. We can't agree with the enemy's words that tell us we're tired and we don't have time. We learn to say "no" and do what's good without giving up. This doesn't come naturally. Only His Spirit activates His truth in us; our task is to submit, get out of His way, and become obedient to His truth. Remember, it's progress not perfection.

What are some huge enemy blockades which keep us ineffective and unproductive? Laziness, greed, selfishness, lies about our worth, self-pity, resentments, and our Goliath—entitlement! We need to check ourselves; is our recovery getting as much time and effort as our drugs, alcohol, or gambling once did? We didn't get tired of doing whatever it took to get our next fix, next drink, or next card. We stood in rainstorms and the freezing cold, and we slept in a car at the casino. If broke, we got money; if sick, we got out of bed. We're now warriors on a crusade to glorify the One who saved us. God's grace enables us to go all in and get as serious in our recovery as we were in our addiction.

We have always wanted a mainline blessing with a sideline commitment. The Advocate activates us off the sideline, exercising His option for us to play. He sends us into the Super Bowl of our new life in Him. He plays through us, and our reward is more than a worldly ring or trophy—our prize is a harvest of blessing in due time!

Lord, I pray for your strength to not get tired of doing what's good and to not give up. I desire to give you the effort I gave my addiction. Thanks for getting me into your game.

Amen.

2 PETER 1:8

What steps did I take to continue using, drinking, and gambling when I was tired? How can I take the same steps when I get tired in my recovery?

THE FATHER REVEALED

I and My Father are one (JOHN 10:30, NKJV).

At the Last Supper, Jesus knew it was His time. His final instructions were to reassure the disciples and prepare them for His death and resurrection. What did the Messiah do? He washed the disciples' feet, providing an example to follow. He told us to love each other as He loves us. Loving our neighbor was taught in Leviticus, but here Jesus commands us to love others as much as He did. This was a total game changer.

We need to discover who our Father truly is. The core for all in recovery is a father issue: we see God the Father in the image of our earthly father. Jesus came to reveal who the Father truly is, so we no longer have to be chained in bondage. In fact, who we think we are does not click with who we think God is. When we agree that Jesus' cross redeems us, then we know who we are and we can live a life free from addiction. God's Spirit convicts us of our sin and our absolute need for a Savior. On our path of recovery, we discover that we spend less time thinking about what creation is doing to us, and more time on what the Creator is doing for us.

God couldn't just forgive us out of love; He gave us His Son out of love. When we personally receive the love of God revealed on the cross, our forgiveness comes and total healing begins. Jesus came to restore us to the Father. We don't just serve a great God, we serve a great Father.

Father, I pray I would drink daily from your river of life. Jesus, thank you for giving yourself entirely to your Father, so we also might be entirely the Father's. Amen.

JOHN 13:1-17, 34, 17:19

How has my relationship with my earthly father
affected my relationship with my Heavenly Father?

HONESTY AND INTEGRITY

*Confess your sins to one another, and pray for one another,
so that you may be healed (JAMES 5:16, NRSV).*

God's spirit guides us to confront our false self and become trustworthy—open to accountability and transparent to grow into who we really are. We must acknowledge our emptiness and how our identity has become twisted. The inability to be totally honest and transparent with others is a giant stumbling block that will sabotage our recovery. God reminds us to trust in Him for strength. It doesn't matter where we've gone; it matters where we're going!

Our dignity and self-respect were stolen by the enemy and by our addiction. Now it's our moment to release our stuff and receive God's stuff. Jesus takes our shame and guilt, the Father forgives, and the Holy Spirit removes. Also, we ask the Great Physician to surgically remove resentments. Do we do a little more work to change? No, we have a little more faith!

Honesty says, "I know the Shepherd's Way"; integrity declares, "I will walk the path He's set before me, consistently." If we desire honesty and integrity from others, we have to be those things to them first.

Lord, I pray you'll fill all my empty spots with your truth which sets me free. Amen.
ISAIAH 41:10; PSALM 51:1; ACTS 19:18

Why am I more concerned about what others think of my confession than I am about my own freedom?

Regular Spiritual Check-Ups

I know about your suffering and your poverty—but you are rich! I know the blasphemy of those opposing you (REVELATION 2:9, NLT).

Pain comes into our lives and suffering threatens our rest and peace. Slander afflicts pain, causing distress that wounds deeply. The danger is to get drawn into the chaos, lies, and deceit with those who attack, belittle, and speak evil over us. When reacting in emotion, we're taking the low road; yet, when allowing God's Spirit in us to deal with mud-slingers, we take a sharp turn to travel the high road where the view is absolutely grand.

We need regular spiritual check-ups: a new discipline essential for growth in our lives. We don't have a good track record of taking care of ourselves physically or spiritually. We need shepherds for accountability. It's difficult at times to recognize this need when we're drifting along, taking things for granted, closed off to encouragement and truth, or relying on ourselves rather than on God. It's okay to ask for counsel, advice, and help with our spiritual examination; we don't let our pride make this decision.

There's no middle ground! We're moving forward with peace and blessings—activated by the Holy Spirit in our relationship with the Creator and Savior—or falling backward out of relationship with God into chaos and curses. Since all sin is relational, we come against slander with God's wisdom.

Lord, thanks for being the rudder of my ship even if I forget at times. I love your high road, and need your Spirit to get me there. Amen.

2 CORINTHIANS 13:5; 1 CORINTHIANS 16:18; PROVERBS 25:21-22

As I examine myself, am I stagnant and heading for relapse or moving forward and heading towards freedom?

FOLLOW HIM OR FOLLOW OURSELVES

I do not consider my life of any account as dear to myself, so that I may finish my course and the ministry which I received from the Lord Jesus, to testify solemnly of the gospel of the grace of God (ACTS 20:24, NASB).

We have a choice to measure our lives by being a reflection of God's grace and be fulfilled, or we can allow ourselves to be tricked into seeking recognition and approval from others, which leads to frustration. "I arise in the morning, torn between a desire to improve (or save) the world and a desire to enjoy (or savor) the world. This makes it hard to plan the day" (E.B. White).

Save the world or savor the world is a challenge to our daily reprieve. Give or take? Respect or disrespect? Forgive or not forgive? Please God or please people? Use wisdom or analysis paralysis? Be truthful or deceitful? Go to a meeting or stay home? Encourage or discourage? Build-up or tear down? Speak words of life or death? Turn our will over to God or do it our way? These are the choices we make to recover or relapse. God says our bodies are not our own while the devil shouts we're just a shack on the other side of the track and claims us to be his. Do we stay with God and drink His living water, or run back to slavery and sip on the enemy's poison?

We follow Him into our destiny and ministry to the best of our ability with His truth lighting the way. We follow Him because we're sick and tired of crawling on the floor following ourselves.

Lord, I rise in the morning expectantly. I pray that I might finish my course with joy and be a reflection of your tender mercy and grace to others. Amen.

LUKE 9:23; 1 CORINTHIANS 6:19; JOHN 16:13; PSALM 119:105

Am I currently following God, the devil, or myself?
What steps can I take to follow God?

My Plans? His Purpose!

People can make all kinds of plans,
but only the LORD's plans will happen (PROVERBS 19:21, NCV).

We can be grateful for our plans that don't work out. Our addiction or self-loathing never allowed us to be content with our present circumstance. We were caught up in the enemy's jig of should, would, and could. Chaos, guilt, and shame ruled our day as people-pleasing greased the skids to lonely, dark places. Everything we've ever experienced—bad, good, stressful, happy, sad, betraying, abusive, encouraging, shameful—God worked everything out for our good.

While God has used our past to get us to where we are today, family members can remain stuck in the muck over our past actions. We have to focus on remaining steadfast in our recovery and take the high road. We courageously put our tennis racket down and walk off the court when they want to play their games. We love them and will be there for them, but their game is no longer ours to play.

As trust in our Heavenly Father grows from a tiny seed, we can know He will turn all our tests into a testimony, creating a beautiful tapestry of His abundant life. Our past was an evil, violent storm which blew all our life's puzzle pieces helter-skelter off the board, but God has diligently and magnificently recovered them all. He can do that for our families, too.

Lord, I pray to meet people, especially family members, where they are. I pray for
the wisdom to know you're working out everything for my good. Amen.
ROMANS 8:28; COLOSSIANS 1:20

Am I able to be truly honest with myself
and realize that my plans have never worked out?

TEARS OF JESUS

Jesus wept (JOHN 11:35, NKJV).

Two powerful words express the profound feelings Jesus, as a human being, had for His friend. Our Jesus of emotions—sorrow and compassion—joined Lazarus' sister, Mary, and others in mourning his death. The Son of God cares enough to weep with us in our sorrow.

We've all come face to face with sorrow in our lives: a death of a loved one, the mental suffering caused by disappointment in ourselves, sadness in our addiction, anguish over circumstances, the darkness and loneliness of depression, or the feeling of rejection or betrayal. Jesus meets us right where we are. He knows our injury and hurt, and when we're weary and heavy-laden, He offers a sanctuary of rest.

Jesus is the example of humility, always following the instructions of His Dad. We can either continue to think we're wise and clever and do things the enemy's way, or we can humbly admit we're poor in spirit and be willing to follow the instructions of our Father.

Lord, Lazarus and I were bound in grave clothes. I am so grateful for the words you spoke over both of us: "Unwrap him and let him go!" Your glory broke our chains of death. Amen.
JOHN 4:34, 11:33-36; MATTHEW 11:28-29

How have my actions affected the feelings of Jesus? What can I do about it?

REMINDERS TO KEEP US SOBER

I intend always to remind you of these qualities, though you know them and are established in the truth that you have (2 PETER 1:12, ESV).

In sports, athletes study film to know their opponents and to improve their game. Coaches devise strategies and game plans that will work specifically against the opponent. The players practice repetitively, even though they know the playbook, and prepare for the coming contest. In school, we study by going over the same material to remind us of the answers so we can pass the test. We need to do this with scripture: review the basics and challenge ourselves to continue building our faith daily! God has an undefeated record, and He wants us on His Dream Team.

We're a member of a team we didn't have to earn a scholarship to play on; in fact, we were chosen to be on this team. The Creator knew our spirit before creation, and He allowed us to be encased in an earth suit for this dimension of life. We chose a life of addiction to medicate our pain, which took us to some extreme ugly places, but the Lord didn't leave us there.

The catch-22 is that God allows us the choice to stumble down our road with blinders on, or to give Him permission to participate and to believe and receive by faith His plans for us. This is why being around champions is so important. We see others walking out their faith in sobriety, and hear how their faith gives them strength to stand firm in the truth. Now we can be those people for others.

Lord, I'm grateful for those whose testimony has reminded me of your strength. Help me to show the same to others who are struggling. Remind me to follow the steps you determined for me. Amen.

EPHESIANS 1:4; JEREMIAH 1:5, 29:11; PROVERBS 16:9

Do I believe repetition is a necessity to keeping me free?

Without God, We're Chasing the Wind

A time to plant and a time to uproot what is planted (ECCLESIASTES 3:2, NASB).

Solomon, with all his wisdom, found that true enjoyment in life came only when following God's guidelines. There is a time and season for everything. Our season of recovery is now! God has given us this window of opportunity to climb through. He provides everything we need to succeed. It's up to us to work out a system, led by the Spirit, that gives us a practical application of God's Word on a daily basis. It's one day at a time. Are we sick and tired of chasing the wind?

Jesus, the Good Shepherd, opens the gate to our recovery; we listen to His voice and follow His lead. We know the thief's purpose is to steal, kill, and destroy. The Good Shepherd wants us to have life in abundance. We never had a clue what our true purpose was. During the many dark, dismal days and weeks in the enemy's torture chamber, he danced and pranced with glee because we had agreed with his lie. He caused us to think we deserved everything he did to us!

We have no obligation to our old sinful life. God's will and purpose for our life is that we aren't dictated to or controlled by other sources. Where do we start? By giving thanks and choosing, today, to respond to the Shepherd's voice.

Lord, thanks for my time and season. I pray for the courage to say no to being a victim, and yes to being victorious. Amen.

ECCLESIASTES 3:1; JOHN 10:3, 10; ROMANS 8:12; 1 THESSALONIANS 5:18

Am I taking full advantage of this opportunity for recovery?

SPEAK TO IT OR SPEAK ABOUT IT

"If you say to this mountain, 'Be taken up and thrown into the sea,' and if you do not doubt in your heart, but believe that what you say will come to pass, it will be done for you" (MARK 11:23, NRSV).

God loves when we choose to make a difference in the lives of others. He is delighted when we sow seeds that feed our starving spirit—when we chew and digest His Word.

Our Messiah endured the violence of the cross and shed His blood to save us. He cancelled our debt, so we can choose a life free from addiction. It's our season to do what He wants us to do. His sheep know His voice; they clearly hear their Shepherd.

We all start with the same faith—God is no respecter of persons. The same initial saving faith He gave Billy Graham and Mother Theresa, He gave to us. We can receive His Holy Spirit through faith. Our challenge is to increase our faith; it's our responsibility, not God's. When we speak the Word, we hear the Word. God gave us the power to speak to our mountains and situations. If we don't speak to them to remove them, we'll continue to speak about them and they will remain.

Lord, thanks for my thirst to hear your Word. I trust your Word that says faith is good for anything today, whatever it is. Amen.

JOHN 10:11; EPHESIANS 2:10; ROMANS 10:10, 17, 12:3; GALATIANS 3:14

Why would I rather complain about my circumstances than give them to God?

HIS WORDS ARE LIFE

"It is the Spirit that gives life. The flesh doesn't give life. The words I told you are spirit, and they give life" (JOHN 6:63, NCV).

The words we speak, and those spoken over us, are liberating or incarcerating. By our words, we set the environment in which we live, and eat the fruit of the words we speak. His Word has to be in our hearts and mouths. Our hearts believe and we're justified; our mouth confesses and we're saved. The enemy hates when we speak the truth. He is out to steal God's Word from us. We say Jesus is our Lord, tell someone they're a loser, and speak death over ourselves almost in the same breath. What intense spiritual warfare! Our recovery depends on words of life.

Abraham was convinced God had the power to fulfill His promise. He had faith to believe what he couldn't see. At the Last Supper, Jesus asked His Father to protect the disciples from the evil one and teach them the truth. We make the decision to believe God's Word, ask Him to participate, and become willing to be instructed by Him. Our sweat equity--speak His Word to hear His Word, often!

God is asking us to untie His hands so He can get involved in our circumstances. He's waiting for us to open our door to His possibilities, to proclaim from our lips that He is Lord, and enter His supernatural rest. We don't need to set ourselves up to fail; we set ourselves up to walk in God's blessings, and He sends His angels to work on our behalf. We need all the help we can get—to decrease that Abba Father may increase.

Lord, I pray to decrease that you increase; I relinquish being in control of my life to now submit, bow, and bend my knee to the power that's in the name of Jesus: my firm and secure anchor. Amen.

GALATIANS 6:7; ROMANS 4:21, 10:8; JOHN 17:17; PSALM 103:20

Why is it easy for me to listen to the devil rather than God?

FOCUS ON TODAY

"Forget what happened before,
and do not think about the past.
Look at the new thing I am going to do.
It is already happening. Don't you see it?" (ISAIAH 43:18-19, NCV)

Some days we allow shame to dictate our present and future. This limits us in being able to forget the past. The miracle that we survived and are alive today gives us another opportunity to recover. Sometimes we declare, "I decided to go to treatment," "I'll never use again," "I have a plan and know what to do." But God giggles and gently whispers, "I got you to this place safely, and desire to show my strength and power through you."

By God's grace we accept our nothingness without Him, and submit to the 24-hour day God has for us. We need to reflect on how far God has brought us. Do we remember our desperation when hitting rock bottom and crying to God for deliverance? There are simply two things that help us receive God's best for our lives: permission and participation. We have no right to expect the promises of God unless we apply His principles.

Learning how to be content, in whatever state we're in, and learning to live on almost nothing is not automatic. Our time is different than God's time. He invites us to be content today. Time gets twisted when we focus on tomorrow or next week. As the importance of our time decreases, time in His presence increases. He specifically chose you and me for His renovation and restoration project.

Abba Father, I give you permission to participate in my life. I watch in hope; I wait for you and know you'll hear me. I pray I wouldn't think about time so much especially when I'm with you. I pray tomorrow does not steal today away. Amen.
PHILIPPIANS 4:13; LUKE 11:3; MATTHEW 6:34; MICAH 7:7

What about my past is dictating my future?

Hang Onto Your Crown

Upon accepting our life was one of disorder and only God can be in control of our recovery, we submit to His authority and receive His crown. We spend so much energy doing things our way, yet God tenderly brings us back to His way. We need to remember how, by His infinite mercy, God reached down into our darkness and guided our feet into the path of peace. The enemy wants to steal our crown and replace it with a counterfeit one.

Jesus also purchased new garments for us with His blood. We know where we're going, but there are times we don't know how to get there; we're afraid with so little faith. We hold back, sometimes putting our big toe into His living water to test what He has for us. God gives us the child-like faith to run off the end of the dock and leap into the blessings of recovery. When the storms of life come, and the waves rise higher, the Lord will make a way.

Doing it our way, we continue to work a half-hearted, half-committed program—one foot in, and one foot out of recovery. Upon discovering we're back on the enemy's roller coaster of control, our Father invites us, once again, to push His recovery reset button. He will cause everything to work together for our good.

Lord, I pray for the courage to hang onto the crown you placed on my head. I'm grateful you clothed me with your garment of salvation. Amen.

PROVERBS 19:21; LUKE 1:79, 17:6; ISAIAH 43:16, 61:10; ROMANS 8:28

Why do I believe what I say about myself or what others say about me, rather than what God says about me?

PERSIST, PERSEVERE, ACT

"Happy are those whose hearts are pure, for they shall see God"
(MATTHEW 5:8, TLB).

As we continue and persist through trials, we discover we're beginning to stand for something greater than ourselves. As the saying goes, "If we don't stand for something, we'll fall for anything." God's grace allows us to keep showing up as what was once unfamiliar becomes more comfortable to pursue. If we don't persist in walking into our freedom, a relapse into bondage of self awaits.

There are many times we can't see past our noses because of our emotion and pride; therefore, accountability with a mentor or sponsor helps us identify the triggers the enemy uses to disrupt our rest and steal our peace. Our mentors also help us discover the motives in our hearts. A hard heart makes for a hard life! With radical trust, we throw away the victim medallion that's been hanging around our neck for years. It's our season to stand for the One who endured the cross for us.

How quickly do we act when God reveals exactly what He desires us to do? Our procrastination needs to be put back where it belongs—in the pit! When we're off His path, we need to get back on it; when we fall, we fall forward; when we're wrong, we admit it; when we need a meeting, we go to it; when we need some rest, we get in His lap. A mentor tells us what we should do; we need to do it even when we're tired.

Lord, I pray you will continue your work on my heart.
I pray for your courage to persist in listening to the mentors you have
placed in my life and to promptly act on their counsel. Amen.
JEREMIAH 3:15; DEUTERONOMY 10:12; PSALM 37:23

In what areas am I becoming complacent in my walk with God?

God's Laundromat

To Him who loved us and washed us from our sins in His own blood
(REVELATION 1:5, NKJV).

The enemy specializes in shame, guilt, and rejection. For many years, he suggested we medicate our pain for relief from yesterday's broken road, today's anxious thoughts, and tomorrow's fear. God's truth declares that we're forgiven for yesterday, strengthened for today, and held in His hands for tomorrow. We can trust He's never forgotten, forsaken, or given up on us, and by His grace we can begin our recovery. Instead of being angry with what we've endured, we can thank Him for bringing us to this day—breathing, alive, and out of prison.

God gives us a new filter to identify how things truly are. We must leave the battlefield of our minds and step into His wisdom. When the enemy comes at us with accusations and condemnation, we know that is not God. We are no longer victims full of self-pity, miserable failures, or condemned prisoners on death row. It has always been His plan to adopt us and purchase our freedom. Why? It gave Him great pleasure.

As a parent, when a child falls into a mud puddle, do we throw away the dirty child or wash the dirty clothes? God sent His Son to wash our mud away with His blood. We need to shed our filthy rags and acknowledge only He can save us. The Lord knows we tried for years, without success, to save ourselves!

Lord, I pray you will continue to wash my clothes as life's dirt and nastiness cling to the fibers. I am grateful for the Holy Spirit who collects and delivers my laundry.

Amen.

PSALM 121:8; ROMANS 8:1; EPHESIANS 1:5-7

What in my current life is in need of washing?

Tell On Ourselves for Our Healing

When I refused to confess my sin, my body wasted away, and I groaned all day long
(PSALM 32:3, NLT).

To groan is to utter a deep sound expressing pain or distress. Our recovery depends on dealing with our grunts and murmuring because they have become our internal language. How many times have we refused to confront our addiction, hiding behind our false self? We're not being picked on. Everyone on this planet, at some time, has agreed with the enemy's lie that if we keep our secret locked inside, it will be okay. This is classic enemy strategy. The truth is that all will be revealed!

Our secrets are not all earth-shattering. Some can be as small as not liking someone but putting on a smile while raging with anger and unforgiveness when you see them. After they leave, we might even express our distress and search for others who agree with us. We justify, make excuses, and continually rehearse the Top Ten Reasons We Don't Need to Confess. This seed, although seemingly small, soon becomes an elephant, opening the door to chaos and another relapse. We don't need to allow the enemy to take us out again!

Only God's Spirit in us can control our bodies, or our bodies will control us. We can't beat ourselves up when we fall into temptation—and we will fall! By God's grace we confess our sin of laziness, criticism, unforgiveness, murmuring, judging, and slander.

Lord, I pray you will draw me back when I wander off your path that is healing my body and strengthening my bones. I pray for courage to be intentional in confessing my faults, even the tiny ones. Amen.
PROVERBS 3:7-8; PSALM 38:3; 1 CORINTHIANS 9:26-27

What am I currently hiding or harboring
that I need to confess in order to receive freedom?

Awake from Our Slumber

I can't help myself because I'm no longer doing it. It is sin inside me that is stronger than I am that makes me do these evil things (ROMANS 7:17, TLB).

God's light reveals that, concerning our choices in life, we're experts at sabotage. We agreed with the enemy's lies that tricked us into becoming our own opponent—subtle self-destruction of living without hope and medicating our shame. Our best intentions couldn't keep us out of the liquor store, crack house, or casino. The slippery slope of self-condemnation, being critical and unforgiving of ourselves, and having an inability to change kept the resentments building and depression deepening.

Only the power of the name of Jesus and His action of love on the cross can deliver us from our slumber. The cunning, slick, double-dealing liar's bleak portrait of our despair and gloom once hung on the wall. It is being replaced now by Jesus' painting of lush green meadows, sprinkled with sparkling white daisies—faith, hope, and love shine forth from the canvas.

There are two kingdoms in all of creation: heaven and hell. Condemnation, sabotage, an unforgiving spirit, despair, and a thousand other tricks to steal, kill, and destroy us are from the pit of hell!

Lord, I pray to embrace more fully the power of your name.
I pray to go deeper with you when I rest in your lap. Thanks for your
new painting of my life; it's absolutely magnificent. Amen.
ROMANS 7:24-25, 8:34

What steps can I take to ask for help and ensure a successful recovery?

HE IS FAITHFUL TO THE FAITHLESS

Our faith may fail, but God will remain faithful. How do we know? We're still alive with the miracle of another chance. In the darkest days of depression, He is faithful! When suicide seems the only option, He is faithful! We seek relief in all the wrong places, and even when we agree with the enemy's lies, God is faithful!

When we could no longer stand, God lifted and held us until we took our first baby steps. He instructed, entrusted, and qualified us to be recruited into His army. When out of service, we complain, snap at others, get angry, and have an opinion about everybody and everything. On the battlefield or in the jungle, a soldier follows the orders of the ranking officer and is on high alert for the enemy.

Wisdom is to know that listening to ourselves is not good. The mind that got us into the enemy's bamboo cage cannot get us out. We need reliable and faithful drill instructors to instruct us on how to be good soldiers and make us aware when civilian affairs begin to entangle us. When we are temporarily captured by the enemy, we should be able to persevere and endure all torture to satisfy and please the one who enlisted us—our Commander-in-Chief, Abba Father.

Lord, I pray for the courage to be faithful when tortured by the enemy. If I have to renounce you to live, I pray for the strength to choose you and die for you. Thanks for always being there for me. Amen.

2 TIMOTHY 2:1-4, 10

What steps can I take to ensure that when my faith is tested, it can be trusted?

Under the Table or at the Table?

Do not love the world nor the things in the world. If anyone loves the world, the love of the Father is not in him (1 John 2:15, NASB).

My power versus God's power—it's a no-brainer, but I can pick me in an instant. Sometimes we plead in the name of Jesus for guidance, wisdom, and direction, and His Spirit empowers us to walk His path; however, our stubborn flesh decides to take the opposite path, regardless of the numerous road signs: Danger, Falling Rocks Ahead, and Dead End. Our pride and ego are revealed once again. We're confused and double-minded; open to prayer but closed to direction and counsel. The Father's love remains in spite of us. He lifts us from the garbage heap. Why do we run back to eat out of the dumpster again and again?

We've got to get this! Our flesh is hostile to God. It has no capacity to grasp spiritual teachings and hates to be told what to do. We experience this at church: goose bumps during the service but before we get to our car the thief has stolen every living word from us. We've sold ourselves short many times, crawling on our hands and knees under the table searching for crumbs while God has already reserved us a seat at His banquet table.

Our Father loves to show off what He can do through recovering addicts. We need to be prepared to know what to do when the gift of a loaded bread truck rolls up to our front step. When we find a crumb, we need to learn how to give it to someone else in need. It's amazing that God takes leftovers like us and makes us overflowing givers rather than takers.

Lord, I love your bread of life. I pray for the grace to come to you rather than relying on myself. Amen.

PSALMS 111:5, 113:7; JOHN 6:35

What in my life is currently taking priority over God?

What do I love more than God?

It Takes a Free Man to Free a Man

Letting your sinful nature control your mind leads to death. But letting the Spirit control your mind leads to life and peace (ROMANS 8:6, NLT).

We set our minds on the flesh or on the Spirit; the consequence of one is lifelessness, the other gives life. We are controlled by our sinful nature; yet, it's not us but the sin in us that is evil and corrupt. Paul struggled with sin just as we do. In our addiction, the enemy deceived us by his counterfeit of truth with a devious strategy of impersonation and double-dealing.

The enemy tricked us into thinking we became the sin we committed, and the only relief from our shame was medicating our pain with drugs, alcohol, gambling, or numerous other addictions. There are two opposing forces: our corrupt nature and our spiritual nature. A mentor, sponsor, or other friends can provide the accountability essential to our recovery: people who love us enough to confront, not coddle, our old behavior. We need to be reminded that when Jesus died, the power of sin died with Him.

Our only hope is in Jesus. He will liberate us from death and free us from slavery. We set our minds on the Spirit so we can have life and experience His peace. It takes a free man to free a man—we share His light of freedom to one who is still suffering.

Lord, thanks for choosing me, for calling me to come to you, for giving me right standing with you, and promising me your glory. Amen.
ROMANS 7:17, 8:30, 37; GALATIANS 5:17; JOHN 8:36

What's holding me back from being brutally honest
and taking direction from my mentor?

IT'S ALL ABOUT OTHERS

If anyone thinks himself to be something, when he is nothing, he deceives himself
(GALATIANS 6:3, NKJV).

The facade of thinking more highly of ourselves than others—a mask we've all worn—sets us up to point out their faults. It's a smokescreen to avoid confronting our shortcomings and to look and feel better about ourselves. It suggests we haven't done enough to qualify for our Father's love, which we know has no conditions. We've been on the outside looking in without hope of ever doing enough. We've believed the lie that it will always be this way. Before recovery, an enemy attack would eventually take us out. In recovery, an attack simply means we're on the right path.

When connected to something greater than ourselves, we begin the process of uncovering all that has been a hindrance for us to accept ourselves. The mask of self-importance is violently ripped off each time we admit we're poor in spirit. To start our healing process, we tell on ourselves. When we tell God, our mentor or sponsor, and ourselves, that we're in dire need of God's grace, the giant of judgment begins to shrink. When we don't judge ourselves so harshly, the judgment of others becomes less. Acceptance of self is the seed for acceptance of others.

God gives us the courage to recognize the person we were: someone in fear attempting to minimize and rationalize our addictive behavior. Now is the time; it's our turn! God instructs us that life is all about others.

Lord, I pray for humility to know that others are as important to you as I am.
I pray for courage to attack any situation with a Bible and be victorious. Amen.

LUKE 12:2; PHILIPPIANS 2:3

In what area of my life do I believe my plan is better than God's plan?

Remember When He Called Us

Even in our sorry state, ready to die for relief and not acknowledging God in the least, He deployed His angels to hunt us down and set us in a safe place. Many of us have been in dire poverty, living in the bleak, barren landscape of depression, while crying out for the Lord to have mercy on us. The devil's deceitful trick of telling us we are lame, blind, paralyzed, anxious, panic stricken, paranoid, or miserable failures are fiery darts that stick deeply.

Hurtful words define us; fear and depression can be huge boulders the enemy keeps piling on. Sometimes there is a depth of dark desolation that leaves us feeling crippled. Sometimes we even considered agreeing with the devil's demand for a blood self-sacrifice, embracing this idea in hopes it would bring relief from the shame and pain.

But God says, "You will not get what you deserve." He washes us clean and renews us every time we relapse—and at times we fall deeper than ever before. God still has a plan and He will see it happen. He will hunt us down and set us in a safe place.

Lord, I praise you for giving me a new life and purpose. I thank you for continuing to hunt me down and set me in a safe place. Amen.
PSALM 31:9-10; HEBREWS 10:23; JEREMIAH 16:16

Am I working a solid recovery program to ensure
I don't have to go back where I came from?

THE ACTION OF LOVE

If we walk in the light as he himself is in the light, we have fellowship with one another, and the blood of Jesus his Son cleanses us from all sin (1 JOHN 1:7, NRSV).

All our sins have been erased because of God's great love for us. We can hardly identify the immense, unfathomable, unconditional love our Abba Father has for us. We need to hear stories of how His love has cleansed others, and we need to observe their actions. People who embrace God's love are great people to be around. When feeling low, we need people in our lives who love us unconditionally.

As we mature, we begin trusting that God could love someone like us. God has ruthlessly and aggressively pursued our hearts to have fellowship with Him. Most of us never knew who God truly was; we had been misinformed by misinformed people. God is love. The blood of His Son cleansed us and saved us for eternity! By His blood, we're not guilty. He recovered us to get us into recovery.

How did we get to this day still alive? Whenever the devil brings our legal case to heaven's court for a verdict of guilty, God asks who will represent us? Jesus stands quickly: "I will, Father. In fact, my blood shed on the cross cleansed all sin—yesterday, today, and tomorrow!" God smiles at how well His Son represented us, and declares throughout the Universe, "Not guilty!"

Lord, I'm so thankful you loved me as the Father loved you and that you desire me to remain in your love. Thank you for being my lawyer when I'm accused of being guilty. Amen.

1 CORINTHIANS 13:7; ISAIAH 61:7; JOHN 15:9

Reflecting back on my life, what are some examples that show me without a doubt that God loves me?

HE MUST BECOME GREATER, I MUST BECOME LESS

"After me comes a Man who has a higher rank than I, for He existed before me"
(JOHN 1:30, NASB).

John the Baptist, while baptizing followers, was asked by the Pharisees if he was the Christ. John told them he was unworthy to untie the throngs of Christ's sandals. The next day, when seeing Jesus, John's purpose was fulfilled when he preached a baptism of repentance for the forgiveness of sins. He gave a simple message: "Repent! The Man is coming!"

As Jesus was coming out of the water, after being baptized by John, the Father confirmed Jesus as His Son and declared that He was pleased with Him. Do we dare follow John's teaching about Jesus becoming greater and us becoming less? Our ego screams, "No way!" The significance of this earth-shattering event continues to unfold with an invitation from Jesus to join His story and make it our story. We can leap onto His train of grace and mercy to our eternal destination.

The Holy Spirit whispers, "Let's wash off the world's filth and remove that which holds you back." We might feel motionless and paralyzed, but if Jesus knew His baptism was extremely important, it should be important to us as well.

Lord, I'm so grateful you didn't throw me away when I was so dirty.
You washed my dirty clothes and gave me a robe of righteousness.
I pray for courage to become less, so you can become more in me. Amen.
MARK 1:4-8; MATTHEW 3:14-15

What is it I need to stop doing or start doing to have more of God in my life?

God Loves to Show Off Through Us

Brothers and sisters, think of what you were when you were called. Not many of you were wise by human standards; not many were influential; not many were of noble birth (1 CORINTHIANS 1:26, NIV).

We collapse from weariness and cry, "God, help me; save me!" He lifts us up and calls us to walk through the door of recovery. God chose us while broken (losers, failures, black sheep); we need to check out why. He even used our dark situations to train us. Now we can pursue our life in recovery with the relentless energy we had for getting to the liquor store before closing time, living in the car at the casino, or waiting for the drug dealer.

Short cuts are setbacks. We need to go all in to receive the actions of Jesus. He erased our debt, cleansed us with His blood, and purchased our ticket to live with Him by His resurrection. This is about transformation of the mind not just renewal. In recovery we ride the roller coaster of emotions; we're on the mountaintop in one instant and in the valley the next. These feelings, suppressed for years, need to be brought to the light. We don't give up. We keep showing up and doing whatever is needed.

Weary and tired from doing it our way, we turn to the One who called us out of darkness. Do we believe God will deliver us? In recovery, all we need to do is give up, give in, and receive what He has for us. God chose us to show off through us! Who else transforms losers into champions and self-centered egomaniacs into servants?

Lord, thanks for saving me, who was once without hope, and giving me hope for others who are still suffering. I am amazed you selected me to love others through me and show off a bit. Amen.

REVELATION 3:8; GALATIANS 6:9; DANIEL 3:17; 1 CORINTHIANS 1:27

How has God recycled the weak and foolish things I've done
to benefit others in their recovery?

ONCE UNLOVEABLE, WE NOW LOVE THE UNLOVEABLE

I waited and waited and waited some more;
Patiently, knowing God would come through for me.
Then, at last, he bent down and listened to my cry (PSALM 40:1, TPT).

Do we remember the exact moment we reached total brokenness? Our life was a mess, and we were drowning in a cesspool, so we cried out to Him to save us from the darkness. God heard us and delivered us. We have to abandon our kingdom of one so we can go boldly to the throne of the Most High God. The enemy and the activities of our flesh had tricked us into bondage and slavery.

We begin to love other suffering addicts because God first loved us. When those around us are tripping out and being disrespectful, we allow God to love them through us—with no shame or condemnation. Why do we struggle loving others who are not loving toward us? Our reactions are a reflection of what we feel about ourselves: we pronounce guilt because we feel guilty; we condemn because we feel condemned; we judge because we're under heavy judgment. Essentially, when we are hurt, we hurt other people.

We need to confront our reaction and response to others using God's principle of love. Our reaction and response is our flesh: dishonoring, selfish, easily angered, and bitter. Our struggle to love others who can't love themselves occurs simply because we don't personally know God's immeasurable, unconditional love and how passionately He pursues us.

Lord, thanks for helping me remember where I came from. While I was unlovable,
you loved me. I pray for the courage to get out of your way so your love can flow
through me to other unlovables. Amen.

1 CORINTHIANS 13:5; 1 JOHN 4:8

Do I have a hard time demonstrating unconditional love?

GOD'S HAMMER OR THE ENEMY'S HAMMER?

"Is not My word like a fire," says the LORD,
"And like a hammer that breaks the rock in pieces?" (JEREMIAH 23:29, NKJV)

His word burns like fire, and is like a mighty hammer that smashes rock? It sounds a bit scary. When we ask the Lord to hear us as we lay our requests before Him in hopeful submission, we might expect a tinker's tiny hammer to do some work, but then God shows up with a fifty-pound sledgehammer!

With sweat on our foreheads and nerves on edge, we ask, "Lord, where are you going to use that huge thing?" He replies, "My beloved, I'm going to answer your prayer, and smash your rock of stubborn resistance." We want to run, yet His gentle voice encourages us to allow Him to hammer away, because His plan is so much better than ours.

Our child-like faith knows our recovery is a lifestyle change. We need to be listening for His words of fire wherever we go. His Word activates our recovery, and when we can't see the way, it reminds us He is the Way. We need help to examine our thoughts and attitudes. This is an extreme challenge for those of us who are egomaniacs or self-centered manipulators. We battle through the flesh to admit it's time to follow direction and be told what to do. The bottom line is our recovery will go well if we seek wise advice and counsel—for everything!

Lord, I pray for courage to ask for help when I don't want to; I'm grateful your
hammer is so much better than the addiction hammer. I love your words of fire.

Amen.

HEBREWS 4:12

What things in my life am I trying to hold together that God is trying to smash? Can I see that these things need to be broken in order for me to be restored?

THE IMPORTANCE OF RESPECT

"These are the ones I look on with favor: those who are humble and contrite in spirit, and who tremble at my word" (ISAIAH 66:2, NIV).

God esteems us when we honor Him. Humility is admitting our absolute need for God, having deep sorrow for doing wrong, and trembling at His Word. Jesus took our disrespect of self to the cross and replaced it with respect of self, so we can respect others. The only way to get respect is to give respect.

Our Father gave us another chance and didn't give us what we deserved because He desired a relationship with us. We show Him great respect when we die to ourselves daily and accept His plan for our lives. To become servants is our spiritual act of worship.

We need an honest evaluation of ourselves that identifies our dire need of God's grace to go another step in recovery. As we honor our Father, we begin to respect our spiritual leaders and imitate their faith. We respect those God put into our lives, to save our lives: a spouse, pastor, brother, leader, friend and foe alike. God has given each of them a position according to their faith.

Lord, I pray a blessing over the spiritual leaders you've given me.
I pray for grace to respect friend and foe alike, imitating how you
meet people right where they are. Amen.
JOHN 3:16; ROMANS 12:1-3, 10; HEBREWS 13:7

Have I lost my gratitude, and how is that affecting
my level of respect toward others?

THE FURNACE OF SUFFERING

*"I have refined you, but not as silver is refined.
Rather, I have refined you in the furnace of suffering"* (ISAIAH 48:10, NLT).

Our pilgrim's journey began the moment we came to the end of ourselves and cried to God to save us. We don't like suffering. We can rejoice through the problems because we know they are good for us. They help us learn endurance.

We have suffered during our addiction and have even gotten comfortable with the dark existence of shame, pain, and guilt. God's wisdom breathes truth into us: He will use the difficulties to refine us. He will help us build character and hope. In Him our future is secure. Without this process, there can't be any progress. He offers to go through it with us, to be there during the refining process especially when it's painful.

We can learn to thank God for opportunities for refinement and growth in the furnace of suffering. It is during these moments of weakness that we learn of His presence—hope anticipating, darkness fading, armed and ready, eyes steady. On our knees we see the bright light in the night. We're no longer alone; we're going home.

Lord, I'm so grateful you're in the furnace of suffering with me. I pray for strength to rejoice a bit more when problems and trials come. Amen.

ROMANS 5:3; PSALM 16:8

What challenges am I currently avoiding because I am intimidated
and think I can't handle them?

THE SEED IS GOD'S WORD

"This is the meaning of the parable: The seed is the word of God"

(LUKE 8:11, NIV).

The Bible is a bag of seeds to fulfill our needs. When we hear God's Word, we need to cling to it, get out of the way, and patiently allow it to produce a harvest. Most of us struggle with impatience while waiting for the proper time to reap our harvest. We have to learn that what was once our time is now God's time. He is never late.

By God's grace, we choose not to give up just before the harvest. We don't need to beat ourselves up for falling short; we just keep moving forward and hanging on tightly until our head hits the pillow. Then we awake to a new day of promise and hope. It's one day at a time. How long are we clean and sober? Today. 24 hours. Alleluia.

Many of us leave the recovery process before any foundation is built and before we experience healing. The distraction of outside influences—phones, relationships, and even children—are examples of people who heard the Word, but couldn't persevere until the season of harvest. We unwittingly surrender our harvest of heaven's shower of blessings. Many will relapse; we need to pray they have another recovery.

Lord, I pray you would remind me, daily, that this is an inside job! I praise you for this active and fertile ground. I pray for your courage to keep weeding the garden, watering, fertilizing, and harvesting the crop you deliver. Amen.

LUKE 8:11-15; PSALM 3:5

When have I gotten ahead of God's time and moved on prematurely?

Our Purpose Comes from Him

I cry out to God Most High, to God who fulfills his purpose for me
(PSALM 57:2, ESV).

Every person on the planet has struggled with the question of purpose. What is our purpose in life? Our addiction took us to places we never wanted to go. Medicating our pain, shame, and guilt kept us locked into a life without purpose. Our flesh was in charge, refusing help. The enemy of our souls kept hammering us with lies: "You're a failure," "you're unworthy of any good thing," "you have absolutely no purpose." We were stuck in the crossfire in the kill zone and spent so much energy trying to get something that could only come from God.

Our best thinking kept us empty and unfulfilled. Sick and tired of our emptiness, and wanting to answer that nagging question, "Whose am I?" we cried out to God Most High. In that moment of confusion, we came face-to-face with the Great Inventor—God the Father. He created us for His own purpose. Inventors know the purpose of their inventions. Since we didn't invent ourselves, we can't know our purpose. God knows; He chose us before we were even born.

We have to trust that nothing we've ever done in our past disqualifies us from His purpose. Like the prodigal son, our Father gathers us in, embraces us tightly, lovingly qualifies us, and makes us right with Him.

Lord, thank you for accomplishing your purpose so I can find mine.
Your purpose was to bring life and peace, and I greatly revere you,
standing in awe of your name. Amen.
PROVERBS 16:4; ROMANS 10:4; MALACHI 2:5

What am I currently seeking to find my purpose in?
Can I accept that God's purpose for me is best?

WHAT IS OUR PURPOSE?

"I have worked hard for nothing;
I have used all my power, but I did nothing useful.
But the LORD will decide what my work is worth;
God will decide my reward" (Isaiah 49:4, NCV).

All of us are recovering from something. For those who are older, recovery can hit a bit deeper. We can be led to think we have lost our identity and our lives are over—just as it sounds in the first part of Isaiah 49:4. God's gift of faith gives us hope when reading the rest of the verse. There is still time!

It's difficult, if not impossible, to be miserable when serving others in need and carrying His message to other suffering addicts. We have get out of our favorite recliner, miss some of our favorite programs, and drop everything to answer a call for help—but it's worth it! We trusted our addiction for relief; we now trust God for our reward. Is our new purpose to get back what we lost? No! Our purpose needs to match His purpose. It's time for us to stop being over-thinkers and instead be over-comers. We don't need a 10-page article of explanation; we wouldn't read it anyway.

This is the moment in time we've been waiting for—whatever our age. It's not too late! We're here! We're alive! We don't have to grieve any longer for what we've lost; we now celebrate what we've gained. This is our purpose: to be shown His power and spread His fame throughout the earth.

Lord, thanks for telling me my purpose. I'm amazed that you spared me, and I didn't
get what I deserved. Amen.

1 TIMOTHY 1:5; EXODUS 9:16

What are things I strived for to find purpose and fulfillment
in which resulted in emptiness?

RUN WITH PURPOSE

I run in such a way, as not without aim; I box in such a way, as not beating the air
(1 CORINTHIANS 9:26, NASB).

Our addictive behavior had us running aimlessly and beating the air when sparring with an imaginary opponent—athletes running a marathon with no finish line. Without purpose, we work our recovery program "our" way being unteachable, lacking discipline, and beating the air. We need to be acutely aware of every step; one wrong step will cancel out the many steps already taken in our new life. We learn how to run with purpose. It's a challenge: we start strong out of the gate, and three weeks into our recovery become complacent and lazy.

God alone examines our hearts, so we should aim to please Him. People-pleasing is a stronghold for many of us. We can either lose favor with people or lose favor with God. We desire to be accepted by others which can dramatically compromise our recovery. God's favor results in fellowship with like-minded people who accept us as we truly are and who will stand with us in the fight. There's no drama or feeling drained after being with them.

God sends us people to teach us wisdom and discipline, encourage us, bring assurance and guidance, help us discover our purpose, and agree wholeheartedly with us.

Lord, I pray for your continued grace to please you, not people. Thank you for my purpose. I'm so grateful you trusted me with my recovery. Amen.

1 THESSALONIANS 2:4; 1 TIMOTHY 1:5; PHILIPPIANS 2:2;
PROVERBS 1:1-6; EPHESIANS 6:22; 1 PETER 5:12

In what areas of my life am I wasting time?

KEEP YOUR HEART

Above all else, guard your heart, for everything you do flows from it
(PROVERBS 4:23, NIV).

We are to be vigilant, alert, careful, and persevering as we guard our heart with intensity. The condition of our heart determines the course of our life, and to protect it we need to be operating on the level in which God has placed us. We may have been teachers in an area, but when God's elevator takes us to a new level, our old ceiling becomes our new floor. He asks us to humble ourselves, once again, to become students of our new environment and receive His training for our new position.

Everything said or done to us, and all we've said or done to others, is stored in our hearts. Our heart runs our life, and it is deceitful and wicked. When hardened, we don't know why we think, say, or do the things we do. Be encouraged, this is an imperfect journey. It may have taken years to admit our lives had spiraled out of control. When we operate in our minds, there is trouble looming on the horizon; that's just the way it is. We absolutely need to ask the Holy Spirit for regular check-ups on our heart's condition to keep it tender. Our flesh hates our Holy Spirit check-ups, and the enemy lies about our heart's condition.

Our Father strengthens us to be vigilant, and declares we're worthy to take care of our new heart transplant. We need a tender heart when we come face-to-face with Jesus.

Lord, I pray to trust you at all times. I continue to pour out my new, tender heart to you. I know you are my refuge. Amen.
JEREMIAH 17:9; 1 CORINTHIANS 13:12; PSALM 62:8

What steps can I take to remove my hard heart
and allow God to tenderize it in order to receive freedom?

CAN OUR HEARTS RECEIVE WHAT THEY ARE HEARING?

We must keep in touch with the condition of our heart, respond when the Holy Spirit whispers a warning that our hearts have grown stubborn, and admit our need to receive a tender, responsive heart. It begins with a decision, continues with examination of self, and culminates when we admit a major overhaul of our heart is essential to our well-being. The only way this will work is when Jesus' blood begins flowing through us—more of Him and less of our control and manipulation. We learn this principle by being held accountable by others.

There will be opposition and counterfeits presented to keep our heart from receiving what we're hearing. The devil will attempt to confuse and distract us so we can't seem to apply what we're being taught. We are to stand firm when our flesh wants to be in control; we dare say "no" to the shame of our past, and "not this time" to the father of lies about our present and future.

We need to examine why it seems so easy to listen to the devil and so difficult to listen to God. We abandon the religion game, brush ourselves off, and get back into the spiritual contest. Remember, this is progress, not perfection. Our Father is there when we walk unsteadily; He upholds us when we stumble. When we know we belong to God, we can hear what He is saying.

Lord, I pray you will delight in my efforts; I'm grateful you make my steps firm. I pray you will continue to watch over my life and keep me from all harm. Amen.

EZEKIEL 36:26; JOHN 8:43, 47; 1 PETER 5:9; PSALMS 37:23-24, 121:7

What in my past has hardened my heart and stops me from receiving God's love?

Heart Condition

"I the LORD search the heart and examine the mind, to reward each person according to their conduct, according to what their deeds deserve"
(JEREMIAH 17:10, NIV).

From our hearts spring our issues. There are things that were in our hearts before we picked up drinking, drugs, or gambling. We don't know how evil our own hearts are. What goes around comes around; what we do, we get! By His grace we no longer need to get what we've always gotten because of our poor choices.

We start by getting out of our flesh and accepting that bad relationships were there because we chose to be in them, and damage was caused while we were using. If we can't admit this, we'll continue to create havoc and injure and hurt others. This isn't just about putting the plug in the jug, setting the crack pipe down, or staying out of the casino; this is about living in freedom. When we think we're doing the right thing, the enemy tricks us for the umpteenth time. It's time to act as if Jesus is walking next to us, because He is!

Our deceitful hearts took us further than we ever wanted to go. We choose not to allow our hearts to make decisions resulting in consequences that we have to make amends for later. What, therefore, are we to do? We submit to the Great Healer and ask Him to perform heart surgery on our stony, stubborn heart.

Lord, I am so ready for your exam, prep, and new heart. I desire to be more tender and responsive. I am excited for your care after surgery. Amen.
PROVERBS 4:23, 21:2; JEREMIAH 17:9; EZEKIEL 36:26

What areas of my life am I currently being deceitful about?

HEART-STONY, STUBBORN

May the Lord lead your hearts into a full understanding and expression of the love of God and the patient endurance that comes from Christ
(2 THESSALONIANS 3:5, NLT).

Our heart and mind craves for God the Father to teach us the core value of being loved unconditionally as only He can. We can approach God as our Daddy and fix our thoughts on His goodness. Only then do we truly know what the Father has done for us. We can enter His room of unconditional love as our stony heart becomes tender.

We were critical and disrespectful of others and ourselves; yet, through multiple treatments and relationship disasters, God continues to offer us the experience of life in abundance through His Son and by His Spirit activating His Word in us. Our Father made us worthy and righteous; He redeemed us. He can direct our hearts into His love if we just get out of the way!

He gives us eternal life; we can't accomplish anything through human effort. Without His Spirit, our blinders remain. God's triple-header reveals truth, lives in us, and gives us the power to respond with a tender heart. He can love those still in addiction through us.

Lord, I didn't know how hard my heart was. I pray my heart remains tender and responsive to your nudging. I thank you for being gentle and humble of heart. When I'm weary, you give me rest. Amen.
PHILIPPIANS 4:8; JOHN 6:63; MATTHEW 11:28-29

What steps can I take to keep God's love in my heart
and prevent hardness from occurring?

SAVED TO SAVE ANOTHER

I will praise You, O LORD, with my whole heart;
I will tell of all Your marvelous works (PSALM 9:1, NKJV).

After our deceitful heart was replaced by our Father's tender and loving heart, we giggled like children knowing that our new hearts had Jesus' blood flowing through every vein and artery. We can't keep this joy hidden inside—His Spirit nudges us to tell others what He's done for us. God is no respecter of persons. What He did for Billy Graham and Mother Theresa, He will do for anyone.

We need to learn and practice the principles essential for living our new life of freedom. The ever present danger is to sabotage our recovery by doing things in our time rather than God's time. We're often blinded by other desires. God has already begun His good work in us; if we leave before He's done, we'll soon be on our path back into the wilderness.

God answered our cries for help. He set us on His rock and showed us that each new day is a great day, regardless of what happens. This is His day for us, not our day for ourselves! Our tests become a testimony about Him, to give hope to others of His marvelous works. God saved us to save another of His kids lost in addiction.

Lord, I pray not to leave my recovery before
you've completed my pathway through the wilderness.
I pray you save another lost sheep through me. Amen.

ISAIAH 43:19

Who is currently benefiting from the fact that God saved my life?

Yes, to Our New Heart

"The LORD does not look at the things people look at. People look at the outward appearance, but the LORD looks at the heart" (1 SAMUEL 16:7, NIV).

How often do we unknowingly embrace a favorite trick of the enemy and judge by outward appearance? By God's grace, we can step into someone else's shoes and walk a few of their steps. We dare to set aside the natural and see the supernatural. We begin to fully embrace that we're poor in spirit and in great need of our Father's love. We submit to the Great Healer and begin to accept ourselves for who God says we are. We receive what He has, and thank Him for what He does through us.

Our tender, responsive heart allows us to become more loving of ourselves which flows to others. As we embark on the marvelous journey into a deeper, more profound personal relationship with the Savior, Jesus holds our new heart in His hands. He begins deleting the devil's programming of our life's computer and downloads His new Spirit in us. As Jesus fills us with Himself, we receive the greatest bonus on this planet—without asking, or being qualified—His audacious gift of replacing our defective blood with the very blood He shed on the cross.

If God checks out our thoughts and intentions today, what will He discover? Is it all about us again, or is it all about Him finally? A stony, stubborn heart's response says we can do things without God. A tender, responsive heart submits to His love and lets Him equip and strengthen it to be used for others.

Lord, I pray for the courage to say yes to my responsive heart.
Thanks for showing me I can't keep what I have unless I give it away. Amen.

2 THESSALONIANS 3:5

If I were to do an honest evaluation of myself,
how would my outward actions not match up with my inward feelings?

Our Heart Valves—Open or Closed?

"What does the LORD your God require from you, but to fear the LORD your God, to walk in all His ways and to love Him, and to serve the LORD your God with all your heart and with all your soul" (DEUTERONOMY 10:12, NASB).

This is what Almighty God, our Creator and everlasting Father, wants from us. How do recovering addicts qualify to become His children? The enemy has twisted us into thinking there is a complicated formula of what we must do. But Jesus already did it! These four essentials are uncomplicated: 1) respect Him; 2) follow Him; 3) love Him; and 4) serve Him. When we're frustrated and exhausted trying to please God, that's our deal! When we ease up, relax, and rest in His lap, it's His deal! God is in charge of the outcome and He wants to write words of life on our hearts.

We know now what's in our hearts and that we've received a new heart. We must store His words in our heart and guard them because it doesn't take much for our hearts to harden. What's stored up in our hearts determines the course of our life and influences our day. There are times when we're having a great day, and out of nowhere a feeling from our dark past hammers us. This is why a spiritual examination of our heart is essential.

God created chambers and valves in our hearts that are properly formed and flexible to fully open or close as needed. How many valves in our spiritual heart are operating fully opened? Are we using our heartbeat for our purpose, or for the purpose of the One who created it? To avoid the ambulance and spiritual emergency room visit, we need to examine and test ourselves.

Lord, I trust you. Thanks for sprinkling my guilt with your blood and cleansing me. I pray for courage to examine my heart. I desire Jesus' shed blood to flow through my heart valves. Amen.

JEREMIAH 17:9; PROVERBS 4:23, 7:1-3; HEBREWS 10:22

Where am I lacking in respecting and serving God?

The Heart Valves of Love and Service

"You shall love the Lord your God with all your heart and with all your soul and with all your strength and with all your mind, and your neighbor as yourself"
(LUKE 10:27, ESV).

The heart valve of love is caring for others. Is there blood flowing? Are our hearts clogged or open? Our addiction destroyed our ability to care for ourselves let alone anyone else. We were in agreement with the devil's stronghold; there was severe judgment and guilt, and we felt unworthy of God's love. We heavily medicated our shame, searching for relief from our pain, as chaos and confusion reigned supreme.

In recovery, we learn to set aside our false pride and ego and receive God's unconditional love, so we can pass it on to those who are hungry, thirsty, and in need of clothes. The truth is that when we serve others in these ways, we're actually doing it for God. But we need to be on guard so we don't get tired of doing good and give up before our reward. As we nurture others, God nurtures us.

The heart valve of service is that we work together to reach a goal that wouldn't be possible on our own. To be new in Christ is to desire to love Him above all else and follow Him wherever He leads. We're no longer alone; we're part of His body. We need to stay close to His heartbeat and be where His fruit is evident. Jesus washed the feet of the disciple who betrayed Him, and He invites us to wash the feet of the very people who have betrayed and hurt us the most deeply. Is this a tall order? Absolutely. Yet when we were filthy and condemned to die, Jesus became our sacrifice—that we might live.

Lord, thanks for placing me so near and close to your heartbeat.
I pray for your grace to have pure motives so my actions will not be hollow—
that they will be God-centered, not self-centered. Amen.

MATTHEW 25:20; GALATIANS 6:9; 2 CORINTHIANS 5:17; JOHN 12:26; 1 CORINTHIANS 12:27

What circumstance in my life is clogging my heart
and not allowing the love of God to flow through me to others?

The Heart Valves of Respect and Trust

Be devoted to one another in love. Honor one another above yourselves
(ROMANS 12:10, NIV).

The heart valve of respect is considering others and preferring them in love. The question we need to ask is are we respecting ourselves and those whom God has placed in our lives as authority? This includes all relationships where someone is in a position of authority over us. Our flesh gets irritated and squirms uncomfortably at any thought of being under authority because it hates being told what to do. What God establishes in Scripture absolutely eliminates any of our excuses!

The heart valve of trust is believing in others. Do we trust those whom God brings into our path? Many of us were mistreated and injured by people we trusted, and we accepted the devil's suggestion of building walls to protect ourselves. By God's grace, we become willing to listen to our spiritual leaders and do what they say. We trust that God placed them in our lives to watch over our souls; they are accountable to God.

Who do we trust? Are we the ones people like to work with or try to avoid?

Lord, I pray for your strength to take up my cross daily and
trust you with all of my heart, so I can learn to trust others. Amen.
PHILIPPIANS 2:3; ROMANS 13:1; MATTHEW 7:12; HEBREWS 13:17; LUKE 9:23; PROVERBS 3:5

What is stopping me from trusting God, myself, and others?
Why do I have a hard time submitting to authority?

IT IS FINISHED

If we confess our sins, he is faithful and just and will forgive us our sins and purify us from all unrighteousness (1 JOHN 1:9, NIV)

This is about fellowship with God the Father and a personal relationship with His Son, Jesus. God already knows what we've done to ourselves and others during our addiction. This is our greatest blessing. Slavery and darkness forced us to surrender and seek His freedom and light. He will not push us away no matter what we've done; instead, He draws us to Himself. Our renewed heart's desire is to have an intimate relationship with our Savior, and do whatever it takes to guard it.

The key is unrelenting honesty—admitting we have sinned. He forgives us and liberates us to confront our flesh when stubbornness, ego, and pride want to rule our day. We have to continually admit our sin to God and other believers. Jesus accepts our human frailties, so we can experiment with accepting ourselves. Are we right with God? The devil will suggest we missed some sins, but God knows our hearts and His blood covers all.

Jesus' ministry, crucifixion, and resurrection are the center of all things in this world. We need to fight, using God's weapons, to keep Jesus in the center of our lives. It is absolutely necessary for our healing. We put our trust in God, whose Son took all our dirt and filth upon Himself and declared, just before He died, that His ultimate sacrifice for the forgiveness of our sins was sufficient. "It is finished," He said.

Lord, I thank you for wiping my slate clean with your shed blood and forgiving my sins: past, present, and future. I pray the brightness of the glory of the Father seen in your face shines on me, my children, and their children. I pray your glory would be magnified in the lives of all who are in recovery. Amen.

2 CORINTHIANS 4:6; 1 JOHN 1:8, 2:12; JAMES 5:16; JOHN 19:30

Why am I letting my past dictate my future?

In recovery myself, and part of a faith-based recovery ministry for ten years, these pages contain essential, yet practical, tools for those who are sick of being sick, and tired of living beneath what God has for them. My love for my wife, Peggy, and our eight adult children, and eleven grandchildren come second only to my love for God. It's God's grace and tender mercy that has gifted me freedom from active addiction to write this devotional journal. My heart's desire is this journal will be your doorway to discover you can never do anything to get God to love you more, or less. His love is unconditional. I pray you experience resting in Jesus' lap as one of His children.

Mike Shea lives in Glenwood, MN and commutes each week to Minneapolis to be part of Serenity Village Recovery and Serenity Village Community Church. He is currently working on his second book, a 365 Daily Recovery Devotional.